A warm toast.
Good company.
A fine wine.
May you enjoy all three.

PAUL DICKSON, *TOASTS*

By Scott Jones

Contributing writer: Steve Pitcher
Inspirations compiled by: Karen Crowley and Joan Loshek
Cover illustration: Dan Brown
Interior illustrations: Roger Gorringe

Acknowledgments:
Page 3 excerpted from *Toasts* by Paul Dickson. © 1981 by Paul Dickson. Reprinted by permission of The Helen Brann Agency, Inc.

Book Division of Southern Progress Corporation
P.O. Box 2463
Birmingham, AL 35201

Created especially for Southern Living At HOME™ the Direct Selling Division of Southern Progress Corporation, by New Seasons™, a division of Publications International, Ltd.

Published by:
Louis Weber, CEO
Publications International, Ltd.
7373 North Cicero Avenue
Lincolnwood, IL 60712

In association with:
Southern Living At HOME™
Vice President and Executive Director: Dianne Mooney
Executive Editor: Susan Carlisle Payne
Wine Expert and Foods Editor: Scott Jones
Copy Chief: Catherine Ritter Scholl
Copy Editor: Jacqueline Giovanelli

For information about Southern Living At HOME™ please write to:
Consultant Services
P.O. Box 830951
Birmingham, AL 35283
southernlivingathome.com

To order additional publications, call 1-800-633-4910.
For more books to enrich your life, visit **oxmoorhouse.com**

Manufactured in China.

8 7 6 5 4 3 2 1

ISBN: 0-8487-2774-6

Contents

A Match Made in Heaven

A fine meal paired with the right wine is one of life's greatest pleasures. But finding the ideal wine for your favorite recipe can be tricky. Sure, you can follow the traditional guideline of white wine with white meat and red wine with red meat. But which red wine? Should you try a Cabernet Sauvignon? A Merlot?

The fact is, any flavorful wine will taste good with food. However, few things can match the culinary pleasure of a perfect food and wine pairing. Finding just the right wine can transform a meal into a masterpiece. So delve beyond the conventional, and open up a whole new world of possibilities. We encourage you to experiment, to break the rules. Taste new wines, and explore unfamiliar recipes! You'll discover pairing wines and foods is more art than science.

As you dive into the hints, tips, and recipes within this book, take a moment to glance at the journal section in the back. These pages will be an essential tool in your food and wine explorations. Record which wine and food pairings earned accolades and which received only ho-hum reviews. You just might discover your favorites among the abundant wines of the world!

In the end, it's important to remember that wine and food are just *part* of a complete dining experience. The pleasure of a meal actually lies in the people and conversation that accompany it. Here's wishing you delicious food, flavorful wine, and lots of friends and family with whom to share both.

Bon appétit!

CHAPTER 1

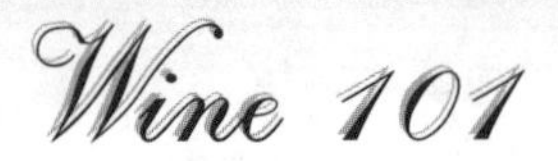

It doesn't take an expert's knowledge to appreciate great wine. After all, it's wine, not rocket science. Here are some simple guidelines to get you started.

Name That Grape

Wines get their names either from the grape that was used to make them (Chardonnay, Merlot, Cabernet Sauvignon) or the region in which they were made (Burgundy, Chianti, Sauternes). Several hundred grape varieties are used to make the world's wines, and each produces a wine that boasts its own unique flavor, personality, and quality. As you find a grape you enjoy, be sure to try several brands because style varies by producer and region. We've listed a few of the most popular grape varieties to help you get started.

Whites

Of all the white wine grapes, Chardonnay is perhaps the most popular. It's generally a deep golden color, which hints that it has been aged in oak barrels. Usually dry, Chardonnay has buttery, fruity, vanilla, and toasty flavors. It pairs well with a host of entrées, including sautéed scallops, chicken in cream sauce, and salmon.

Sauvignon Blanc is a dry white wine that's lighter in color and body and more citrusy and herbaceous than Chardonnay. It's a food-friendly wine with an acidic zing. Sauvignon Blanc's crisp, grassy flavors pair well with spicy dishes and grilled fish.

Riesling—sometimes called White Riesling or Johannesburg Riesling—displays aromas and flavors that range from flowery to fruity to hints of minerals. Riesling is generally considered a sweet wine, though it's often dry. This is a light-bodied, refreshing choice for spicy, salty, or smoked dishes.

Rosé falls into the white wine category, though it sometimes has the crossover potential of a light-bodied red. Also called "blush" or "pink," good quality rosés are made using red grapes. Before fermentation, the skins are given limited contact with the grape juice, thereby producing a wine that is pink in color. Rosé is served chilled and—with its relatively low alcohol and refreshing acidity—is particularly good during the summer.

Reds

Cabernet Sauvignon is a deep, rich, ruby-red wine with peppery, berry, and vanilla qualities from oak aging. "Cab" pairs well with beef, poultry, pasta with red sauce, and game meats.

Zinfandel is one of the original grapes of California and ranges in style from medium to full bodied. Known for its ripe berry flavors and deep crimson color, Zinfandel is often produced from vines that are more than 40 years old. It pairs well with grilled meats, especially lamb.

Merlot is one of the more popular red wines—especially among those who enjoy fruitier flavors (but not necessarily sweet) and less tannic taste. (Tannin is an astringent substance in grape skins, stems, and seeds that makes your mouth pucker as you sip.) Merlot has a deep ruby color but is a softer, more subtle wine than Cab. Its flavor can hint of berry, black cherry, plum, spice, and tobacco. It pairs well with poultry and lamb.

Pinot Noir is more delicate than either Cab or Merlot. Hints of spicy cherries with earthy nuances create a complex flavor. It pairs well with beef and ham.

A Word About Blends

Most wines—both white and red—are a blend of more than one grape. Of course, there are exceptions to the rule. Often, a certain growing location requires that only one grape be used, and other times the grape is simply the choice of the producer, which is usually stated on the label. In most wine-growing areas, there are specific laws determining how much blending can take place before a wine is no longer

Shopping for Wine

If you've ever browsed the wine aisle of the grocery store, you know there are many different wines out there. But don't let that intimidate you. Follow these simple steps for a pleasant shopping experience:

- Find a wine shop where you feel comfortable. If you feel intimidated, your buying experience will be far from enjoyable. Try to establish a relationship with a clerk or two; this will make you feel more comfortable about asking questions.
- Tell the clerk the price you want to pay.
- Describe the kind of wine you prefer. Don't get hung up trying to speak the language of the wine clerk. Use whatever descriptive words you prefer to describe wine—soft, sweet, spritzy, tart, fruity.
- Mention the kind of food you plan to serve with the wine.
- Ask for a tasting sample, if available. Weekly wine tastings at supermarkets and wine shops are a great way to discover what you like.

Cabernet Sauvignon or Chardonnay, for instance. However, within those laws, winemakers will mix wine from other grapes to soften, balance, or add structure to the dominant grape being used. For example, Merlot is often blended with Cabernet Sauvignon to soften the tannic taste, though the label will still read "Cabernet Sauvignon." Blending in this manner is done for a range of reasons, but staying with a consistent style or house signature is one of the most important.

The "blends," or combinations, you see in wine stores (especially from producers in Australia, Argentina, and California) are something much different. These blends—with the grapes clearly marked on the label—are usually limited to two

In a Restaurant

In many restaurants, the waitstaff is coached on recommended wine pairings for specific menu items. Let them know your price range and what you're having for dinner. If you and your guests are eating different foods, you can either compromise on a bottle of "all-purpose wine," such as a light red (not too sweet or too acidic), or order by the glass. Purchasing a bottle is usually cheaper than buying by the glass.

When your server brings the bottle to your table, examine the label to verify that it's what you ordered. If you're given the cork, make sure it isn't dried out or crumbly—a sign of improper storage or previous opening. Next, the server will pour a sip of wine. Swirl it around in the glass, smell it, and taste it. If it smells "off" or tastes vinegary, send it back—but don't return it just because you don't like it as much as you had hoped. After your approval, the waiter will serve others at your table.

(sometimes three) grapes, with Shiraz and Cabernet Sauvignon (red) and Chardonnay and Sémillon (white) being the two blends you'll see most often. The percentages of the respective grapes are listed on the label with the majority of the blend being comprised of the grape listed first. Sampling blends is a great way to discover what you like in a more specific way. Most are less than $12, so they tend to be great values.

A Little Bit of Sparkle

All Champagne is sparkling wine, but not all sparkling wine is Champagne. For a sparkling wine to be called Champagne, it must be made with specific grapes from the Champagne region of northern France. In other words, if you pick up a bottle of sparkling wine with the word

"Champagne" on its label and it's not from France, put it down.

As a rule, the phrase you're looking for on a label is *Méthode Champenoise,* which means that the wine is made in the *style* of Champagne. Delicious and affordable sparkling wines are made all over the world. In fact, every wine-producing country in the world has a region devoted to producing sparkling wine. The most widely available and affordable sparkling wines are made in the United States, Spain, Italy, and Australia.

Italians produce a couple of sparkling wines, notably Prosecco, from the Veneto region (home of Venice), and Asti (formerly Asti Spumante), from the Piedmont region.

Spain's wonderful sparkler, Cava, is made in the Penedés region near Barcelona. It can often be found for less than $10.

Serving Savvy

Wines reveal their best qualities when served correctly. The cork must be extracted properly; the bottle must be at an optimum temperature; the wine must be served in an appropriately shaped glass. In a way, this can be as much of an art as selecting the perfect wine.

Temperature Check

There's no question that serving temperature can either aid or work against your enjoyment of a particular wine. To taste fresh, wine should be served at least a few degrees cooler than the temperature of the room in which it's to be enjoyed. A cooler temperature helps bring out the wine's flavor and bouquet. That said, most reds are best served at cellar temperature, which is somewhere around 62 to 65 degrees Fahrenheit. Before popping the cork, you can put a bottle in the refrigerator for ten minutes or so to bring the wine to the correct temperature. But watch the clock—overchilling red wine can exaggerate the tannic taste and slow the development of the bouquet. If it happens to get a bit too cold, set the bottle out a few minutes before you plan to serve it; the wine will warm quickly as the meal gets under way.

White wines, on the other hand, should be served a little cooler than reds, at around 58 to

62 degrees Fahrenheit. There's a tendency to drink or serve white wine that's ice cold. Avoid this, if possible. White wine that's too cold will taste flat and lifeless.

Champagne and sparkling wines are best served very cold, around 40 to 45 degrees Fahrenheit. Cool the bottle in an ice bucket and serve in chilled glasses.

To Decant or Not to Decant

There is always a question of when to decant, which means to pour the wine from the original bottle to another container before serving. There are several reasons for decanting wine: when an older wine contains sediment, when you wish to improve the bouquet and soften the taste of a young red wine, or when there are broken pieces of cork floating in the wine.

If you decant wine, it's probably best to do so near serving time. To decant a young wine, pour it into the decanter rapidly so that the wine will splash up the sides and incorporate more air. To decant an older wine with heavy sediment or a crumbling cork, place a funnel in the neck of the decanter, line it with cheesecloth or muslin, and slowly pour through the funnel, stopping as soon as the sediment begins to appear. You can also decant an older red wine by placing a flashlight or candle beneath the bottle as you start to pour so you can clearly see the sediment as it approaches the neck. Stop pouring as soon as you see the dark sediment.

Opening the Bottle

Wine should be opened gently with an opener that enables you to extract the cork cleanly and smoothly. Most young red and white wines are very simple to open. But you must take more care when removing the cork of an older red wine to avoid disturbing the sediment in the bottle. Champagnes and sparkling wines must also be opened gently to prevent the cork from flying off and to keep the wine from bubbling over.

Whatever its cost or design, a wine opener should have an evenly coiled, smooth screw that will enter the cork without causing it to break or crumble. A two-pronged extractor is a little more difficult for most people to use, but it does remove the cork without actually piercing it, which is helpful if you wish to reuse the cork.

To open most young red or white wines, stand the bottle upright and cut around the foil just below the protruding part of the bottle top. Remove the foil so it will not touch the wine as it's poured. Then insert the screw of the opener into the center of the cork, twisting slowly. When the screw is firmly embedded, carefully pull out the cork. Be sure to wipe off the rim of the bottle before serving or decanting the wine. If serving directly from the bottle, twist it gently as you pour to prevent dripping.

Before opening an older red wine that contains sediment, place it upright for a day or two to allow the sediment to settle to the bottom.

Fill ev'ry glass,
for wine inspires us
And fires us
With courage, love, and joy.

JOHN GAY,
THE BEGGAR'S OPERA

When removing the cork, move the bottle as little as possible. If the bottle hasn't been allowed to stand upright, serve it from a wine cradle so you won't disturb the sediment as you pour.

Champagne and sparkling wines are less likely to explode and bubble over upon opening if well chilled. But even if the Champagne is cold, it must be opened with caution. Start by peeling back the foil wrapper and exposing the wire cage or muzzle. Unwind the wire with one hand while holding the cork down with the other; then remove the wire. Still holding the cork, angle the bottom of the bottle toward your chest and the neck away from guests or breakable objects. Grasp the cork with one hand, and twist the bottle gently with the other hand. As added insurance, place a napkin over the cork.

Wine Glass Class

In a perfect world, you would own a wide selection of glasses to suit each particular style of wine (red, white, sparkling, dessert, fortified, etc.). A basic white wine glass has a tulip shape, whereas a glass for red wine has a larger balloon shape. Champagne or sparkling wine glasses have long flute- or tulip-shaped bowls so you can see the rising bubbles. Fortified wines, such as Sherry, Port, or Madeira, are served in smaller, tulip-shaped glasses that are narrow at the rim.

However, for the vast majority of wine drinkers, one thin, clear, all-purpose wine glass (whether tulip- or balloon-shaped) with a capacity of 10 to 12 ounces will do. The one exception is the Champagne flute. Its narrow shape concentrates the wine's bubbles and bouquet, and the limited capacity of the glass (between four and eight ounces) helps maintain the Champagne's temperature.

When serving wine, don't fill glasses more than halfway. The remaining space allows for swirling and the development of the wine's bouquet. Again, sparkling wine is the exception to the rule. Because its bouquet is developed from the bursting bubbles rather than from swirling, the glasses can be filled almost to the top.

A Matter of Taste

Your sense of smell plays a major role in sampling and selecting wines. That's why, however dramatic it may seem, there is merit in carefully swirling the wine and sticking your nose right in the glass. The wine coating the inside of the glass evaporates, releasing its *aroma* (the actual smell of the wine) and its *bouquet* (the smells created by the winemaker during fermentation and aging). Aroma is often associated with the smells of fruits—for instance, apples, pears, and pineapples in white wine and berries, cherries, and plums in red. Oak-barrel aging influences the bouquet with smells of vanilla and coconut.

To swirl the wine, grasp the stem of the glass rather than the bowl (so you don't raise the temperature of the wine with your hands). Set the glass on the table, and swirl it cautiously. Then bring the glass quickly to your nose, breathe deeply, and savor a sip. The scents you detect depend on the type of grape used, where it was grown, if the wine was aged in oak barrels, and how long it has been bottled. The key is to connect the smells in the glass with those in your memory. Think cut grass, fruits, vegetables, spices, flowers, burnt toast, leather.

Saving the Rest for Later

The key to preserving an opened bottle of wine is to limit its exposure to air. In scientific terms, it's all about oxidation. You know how an apple or a banana turns brown once it's peeled? Well, a similar thing happens to wine. Prolonged exposure to oxygen is wine's number one enemy. You can recork the wine, but the seal won't be very tight, and the wine will not last for more than a day or two.

The most economical way to keep an opened bottle around for more than a couple of days is to use a hand-pump vacuum sealer (available in kitchen sections of most department and grocery stores for about $12). The sealer uses a one-way rubber stopper that does a pretty good job of removing excess air from the bottle. It's best to store leftover wine in the refrigerator, which also helps reduce spoilage.

Another option is to freeze leftover wine in ice cube trays. Store the frozen wine cubes in plastic bags in the freezer for later use in soups, stews, and casseroles.

CHAPTER 2

Wine Wonderings

Still find this world of grapes confusing? Don't worry, even the experts get confused from time to time. We've provided a sampling of frequently asked questions to help demystify wine and make your experience all the more enjoyable.

Q: How do varietals like Merlot, Cabernet Sauvignon, and Pinot Noir rank in degree of intensity and flavor?

A: Grapes are generally ranked in what is commonly called the "tower of power," which classifies softer, less tannic wines at the bottom and works its way to the top with the most full-bodied and tannic grapes.

Beginning at the bottom of the "tower" are grapes such as Gamay (found in the easy-drinking wines from Beaujolais) and its Italian counterpart, Dolcetto. Wines made from these grapes are low in alcohol, high in acidity, and very light bodied.

The next level is comprised of grapes such as Pinot Noir and lighter-styled Merlots, grapes that are good with roasted or grilled chicken and pork, for example.

Moving up, you'll find medium- to full-bodied examples of Sangiovese and Zinfandel (though oftentimes Zinfandel can be the most full-bodied wine in the room, particularly one with a higher alcohol content). Close to the top are full-bodied Cabernet Sauvignons, followed at the top by Syrah (referred to as Shiraz in Australia), grapes usually reserved for hearty steaks and grilled lamb chops, for example.

Q: **I've heard there are some foods that can affect the taste of wine. Is this true?**

A: There are, in fact, a few food and wine combinations that are a bit tricky. Foods that are very spicy or smoky in flavor (i.e., curry dishes, smoked meats, grilled or roasted beef and poultry with spicy crusts and sauces) can simply overpower a wine. In addition, a common ingredient in spicy foods is salt, which ends up emphasizing the taste of alcohol (particularly in wine with an alcohol content above 11 percent). Combat this by serving white and red wines higher in acid and fruitier in flavor (but not necessarily sweeter). Think about the classic

pairings of caviar or smoked salmon with Champagne (salty and smoky items paired with a cool, acidic wine). In the case of red wines, it helps to serve them somewhat cooler than usual, to bring out the acidity.

Fatty fish also present a problem in the presence of highly tannic red wine. Fish such as salmon and tuna are high in Omega-3 oil, which, when combined with tannic red wine, gives both fish and wine an unpleasant, metallic flavor. However, this is not to say that red wines can't be served with fish. Red wines with low to moderate tannins and relatively low alcohol content will do just fine. Look for wines such as Beaujolais (made with the Gamay grape), Pinot Noir (from Burgundy or the United States), and the Italian gem, Dolcetto.

***Q:* I get a headache every time I drink red wine. I've been told it's the result of sulfites in the wine. Is that true?**

A: This is perhaps one of the most misunderstood topics among wine drinkers. Even before the 1988 federal law requiring all wine labels to read "contains sulfites," all wines contained sulfites. They're natural by-products of fermentation. Throughout history, winemakers have added a small amount of sulfites (sulfur dioxide) to wine, particularly white wine, to prevent oxidization and spoilage. Red wine, on the other hand, contains tannin, which is a naturally occurring preservative in the grape's skin. So, there's even less need for additional sulfites.

Most research now shows that headaches are likely the result of a person's inability to metabolize red wine rather than a reaction to sulfites. Also, to some degree, the headache may be an allergic reaction to the histamines in red wine, though the level of histamines is relatively low.

Q: What's the difference between Chardonnay and Sauvignon Blanc?

A: Chardonnay is generally made in a medium- to full-bodied style (ranging anywhere from big and oaky to dry and acidic). On the other hand, there's the lighter styled Sauvignon Blanc, known for its crisp acidity and clean fruit flavors. Chardonnay, though produced widely in America and the Southern Hemisphere, is the classic grape of Burgundy. Sauvignon Blanc, also a popular grape in California (where it is often referred to as Fumé Blanc) and New Zealand, is the classic grape of Bordeaux and the Loire Valley. Chardonnay is usually paired with more assertive recipes using such meats as pork, chicken, and veal (especially when grilled or roasted). Sauvignon Blanc is the perfect summertime match for items such as shellfish and goat cheese.

Q: What is Sherry, and where is it produced?

A: Sherry is a fortified wine made in southwest Spain, specifically in Andalusia. Fortified wine is made when neutral brandy is added to a wine to raise its alcohol content. Other fortified wines include Port, Madeira, Marsala, and Vermouth.

There are five basic styles of Sherry ranging from dry to sweet: Manzanilla, Fino, Amontillado, Oloroso, and Cream. Manzanilla and Fino should be served chilled with appetizers, whereas Oloroso and Cream are served after dinner, at room temperature.

***Q:* What exactly is Shiraz?**

A: Shiraz is the Australian version of the classic French grape Syrah, long associated with France's northern Rhône growing region. The grape found its way to Australia in the 1830s. Today, Shiraz is the country's leading red grape variety. Shiraz is quite popular in America because of its great value and its slightly sweet, full-bodied flavors of black pepper, blackberry, and raspberry. Shiraz is typically sought as an alternative to Cabernet Sauvignon. There are plenty of good examples of Shiraz; here are a few favorites: Jindalee, Murray-Darling, Rosemount Estate, and Lindemans "Bin 50."

Q. What are people referring to when they say a wine has good "legs"?

A: A wine does have "legs" (also referred to as "tears"); however, contrary to what you may hear around the table, this isn't an indication of the wine's quality. The tiny streams of wine that line the glass as it's swirled simply give you an indication of the wine's power, which is based on alcohol, sugar content, and glycerol (a syrupy substance that's a by-product of the fermentation process). Thick, slow-moving legs indicate a full-bodied wine that's either high in alcohol or very sweet, particularly in the case of dessert wines. Low-alcohol, light-style wines have thin, fast-moving legs.

Q. What's the connection between Beaujolais Nouveau and Thanksgiving?

A: On the third Thursday of every November, the new vintage of Beaujolais—Beaujolais Nouveau—arrives from the southern part of France's famous wine-producing region of Burgundy. However, don't confuse this easy-drinking red wine from Beaujolais (made with the Gamay grape) with the red wines of Burgundy (made with Pinot Noir). Beaujolais Nouveau explodes with fruit flavor, boasts a ruby red color, and contains only a trace of tannins. In addition, a slight chill on the wine helps to bring out its wonderful fruitiness and acidity. Because of its annual release date, value (most Beaujolais Nouveaus cost about $8), and approachability, it has become a Thanksgiving staple right alongside the turkey and dressing. Beaujolais Nouveau is meant to be consumed within six months of its bottling.

CHAPTER 3

A Perfect Pair

Food and wine are a culinary match made in heaven. Although there are acknowledged customs regarding the pairing of food and wine, there are no hard-and-fast rules. You can follow some traditional guidelines, or you may find it more enjoyable to experiment on your own. Whatever your approach, you're sure to discover some wonderful, harmonious food and wine matches.

Making a Match

Before you begin the selection process, repeat the following phrase to yourself: "Serving wine with food should be a simple, pleasurable experience." It's easy to become so overwhelmed with the vast number of wine choices that you feel you must research and analyze each selection to the point of allowing it to become a burden. Where is the fun in that? On the other hand, you don't want to put time, thought, and love into planning a meal and then choose any old wine to accompany it. The challenge here is to strike a balance in which your wine decision is not taken too seriously nor made too hastily. In the end, the best wine and food matches are usually achieved when a happy, middle-of-the-road attitude is taken toward selecting the wine.

There are several different approaches to pairing wine with food. First, recognize that the concept of white wine with white meat and red wine with red meat is rather limiting and fails to take into consideration some of the other key elements that should influence your selection. Always keep these specific points in mind:

- What is the main ingredient in the recipe?
- Does the dish include a sauce? If so, what is the base or flavor of the sauce?
- Are there any other flavoring agents? For example, is the dish salty or highly seasoned with herbs?
- How was the dish prepared? Was it sautéed in butter or grilled, smoked, or simmered for hours?
- Will the food be served hot or cold?
- What kind of wines are available to you, and what price range fits your budget?

For example, when selecting a wine for Cornish hens, consider whether they're to be baked and basted with butter, rubbed with salt, coated with herbs, served with a sauce, or charred on the grill. Any of these procedures could dramatically alter the taste of the hens and thereby influence your wine selection.

As you consider each of these elements, let your thoughts progress to the point where you base your final selection on one of the following concepts: sameness, contrast, or intensity. Keep in mind that these are merely guidelines and will not automatically lead you to the perfect wine and food match. Use them as a starting point for the selection process. The ultimate choice should be based on a combination of factors. The challenge lies in determining what makes the best match for each individual food and wine.

Sameness

To select a wine based on the concept of sameness, simply pair wines with foods that seem to have the same or similar characteristics. For example, match a rich lobster dish with a richly flavored white Burgundy; a lightly sauced chicken dish with a light Chardonnay; an earthy beef-and-mushroom dish with an aged, earthy Pinot Noir or a red Bordeaux; or a sweet dessert with a sweet Sauternes. This is the simplest approach to food and wine pairing. After all,

Pairing Cheese and Wine

CHEESE	WINE
Asiago	Full-bodied reds
Brie	Most reds; medium sweet whites; sparkling wines; cream Sherries
Camembert	Most reds and whites
Cheddar, mild	Most whites or rosés
Cheddar, sharp	Full-bodied reds
Chévre	Full-bodied reds
Feta	Light reds; medium sweet whites
Fontina	Dry reds; for milder versions, most whites
Gouda	Most whites or reds; Sherries, Ports
Havarti, Danish	Dry reds or whites
Jarlsberg	Most wines
Monterey Jack	Most wines
Mozzarella	Dry reds or whites
Muenster	Light reds; rosés; dry whites
Parmesan	Dry reds or whites
Roquefort	Reds
Stilton	Ports
Swiss	Most reds or whites

when food and wine have similar flavors and characteristics they won't overpower each other. However, if the wine and food taste *too* much alike, the pairing may become boring. Sometimes too much of a good thing can be hard to take.

Contrast

The second concept—contrast—can be responsible for many exciting wine and food matches. A salty cheese served with a sweet wine, such as a Sauternes or sweet Vouvray, can make a fabulous combination. Or pair a crisp, dry white wine like Pinot Grigio or a dry red wine like Valpolicella (an Italian red) with fish. The acidity will serve the same purpose as a squeeze of lemon juice and will cut any strong taste.

But contrast must be practiced with caution. Sometimes the food and wine will contrast so much that the tastes fight each other and a pleasant match is impossible. The key to using the sameness and contrast concepts is to plan and anticipate in your mind which matches will be more harmonious. It's obviously to your advantage to have a good idea of the true flavor of the food from having prepared and eaten it in the past. It's also best to make your wine selections from wines you have sampled before; otherwise, you may prefer to seek the advice of a more experienced taster.

Serving Dessert Wines

To those who make a living fussing over wine, this is actually a pretty complicated subject. However, for those of us simply looking for a great wine and food experience, it's pretty easy. All you have to do is remember one simple rule: Make sure the wine is sweeter than the dessert.

Sugar, by nature, tends to deaden the palate. So if a dessert is loaded with sweetness, you'll lose the wonderful nuances of the wine. That said, it's probably best to select fruit-based desserts (fruit tarts, for example). You'll also want to avoid desserts with rich cream sauces, even if the sauce isn't that sweet. The goal is to give the wine a chance to work in concert with the dessert.

Serve dessert wines cold. They're fairly high in alcohol, so keep an eye on how much you pour—you want to fill each glass with about two ounces.

Intensity

The third concept, intensity, revolves around the idea that simple wines require simply flavored foods, and assertive wines can support highly spiced foods. This makes sense because a wine that has a strong, bold flavor can overwhelm a mild dish so that the food would seem to have no flavor at all. The opposite could occur if you paired a delicate wine with a robust dish. So, you might serve a bold wine with a spicy Indian or Szechwan dish or a mild wine with a delicately sauced French dish. However, selecting a bold wine for a bold dish doesn't guarantee a harmonious, tasty match; exercise care and make sure that the wine and food pairing is based on more than just intensity.

Order, Order

Making a match becomes more challenging if you're selecting a wine or wines for an entire menu rather than for just a single dish. Keep in mind that the success of any match within a menu will be influenced by the preceding course and the wine that was served with it.

The best approach to take when planning wines for an entire menu is to begin by analyzing the wines for sweetness. Plan to serve your driest wines first and progress to the sweeter wines. Also, consider the color of the wines. You should serve white wines before light red wines, light red wines before dark red wines. Another way to look at the progression would be to serve the younger wines first and the older wines last.

Specific situations could force changes in these serving ideas, but for the most part the guidelines are logical and practical. Sweet wines, particularly Sauternes, which is traditionally served as an appetizer wine or a dessert wine, are an exception. Some floral Champagnes may also work well when served with dessert. An exception may also be necessary depending on the

season. Heavy red wines aren't as pleasant served in the heat of summer as are light white wines. And the opposite case occurs in winter; the taste for red wines seems to thrive on cold, wintry days.

Now You're Cooking

As you explore ways to marry wine and food, remember that wine is one of the most useful cooking condiments around. Use it to tenderize meat or to add wonderful flavor to a marinade. As with other aspects of wine and food pairing, however, there are a few things to consider if you want to avoid a disaster in the kitchen.

Quality First

Never cook with a wine you wouldn't drink. It's tempting to try to save money by purchasing lower-quality wine with which to cook, but remember the taste of the wine is just as important in cooking as it is in drinking. This doesn't mean you have to cook with the most expensive wine in the house. It does mean that you'll want to avoid that open bottle of wine that's been in the refrigerator for two weeks. And by all means, avoid

anything labeled "cooking wine" (which is produced from bottom-of-the-barrel wines and made even more insipid with the addition of salt).

Compliments to the Chef

You want to cook with a wine that best complements the recipe. Just as you select the proper style of wine for an appropriate food, so too should you use the same approach in the kitchen. For example, delicate poached recipes are best when a delicate wine is used. It's important to remember that as the wine cooks, its various flavors intensify. So for savory dishes, stick with wines that are relatively dry (not too sweet). In addition, avoid wines dominated by oak, which can add an unpleasant bitterness.

Many chefs use a technique called "bridging," in which they cook with the wine they plan to serve. This "bridge" allows the flavors in the sauce to be highlighted in the glass. Simplify the wine and food equation by using this method in your own kitchen.

For more suggestions on pairing wines with food, refer to the chart and recipes that follow.

Wine & Food Pairing Chart

(Wines listed by grape variety are in regular type; regional varieties are in italics.)

FOOD	WINES
Hot, spicy foods **Ingredients like:** chiles, ginger, and pepper **Common cuisines:** Chinese, Indian, Mexican, and Thai	**Slightly sweet, fruity, light wines** such as *Beaujolais*, *Burgundy*, Chenin Blanc, Gewürztraminer, Pinot Noir, Riesling, *Rhône wines,* Sauvignon Blanc, and light Zinfandels
Acidic, tart foods **Ingredients like:** citrus, feta cheese, garlic, lemon, tomatoes, vinegar **Common cuisines:** Creole, Greek, Italian, and Japanese	**Highly acidic wines** such as Chardonnay, *Chianti*, Sauvignon Blanc, and sparkling whites
Rich foods **Ingredients like:** butter, cheese, lobster, red meats, and salmon **Common cuisines:** French, German, Italian, and Southern	**Acidic, citrusy wine** such as Sauvignon Blanc **Oaky, toasty, buttery wine** such as Chardonnay **Tannic (tart), darker reds** such as Cabernet Sauvignon, Merlot, and dark Zinfandel

Wine & Food Pairing Chart (continued)

FOOD	WINES
Salty or smoked foods **Ingredients like:** olives, salt-cured or smoked meats, and soy sauce **Common cuisines:** Japanese, German, Greek, and Southern	**Slightly sweet, fruity light wines** such as *Beaujolais*, Chenin Blanc, Gewürztraminer, Pinot Noir, Riesling, sparkling wines, and light Zinfandels
Sweet foods **Ingredients like:** coconut, corn, fruits, mint, and thyme **Common cuisines:** Chinese, French, Indian, and Thai	**For foods other than desserts: slightly sweet wines** such as Chenin Blanc, Gewürztraminer, and Riesling **For desserts: sweet wines** such as Madeira, Ruby Port, *Sauternes*, Sherry, and sparkling wines such as *Asti* (formerly Asti Spumante) **Note:** Pair sweet foods with sweet wines, but the food should never be sweeter than the wine.

Red Pepper Hummus

- 1 (15-ounce) can navy beans, rinsed and drained
- 2 garlic cloves, chopped
- ½ cup roasted red bell peppers, drained and chopped
- ⅓ cup tahini
- ¼ cup fresh lemon juice
- ¾ teaspoon salt
- ¼ teaspoon ground cumin
- ¼ teaspoon ground coriander
- ¼ teaspoon ground red pepper
- 2 tablespoons olive oil
- 1 tablespoon chopped fresh cilantro
- Garnishes: lettuce, toasted sesame seeds, chopped green onions

PROCESS first 9 ingredients in a food processor or blender until smooth, stopping to scrape down sides. With processor running, pour oil through food chute in a slow, steady stream; process until smooth. Stir in cilantro; chill 1 hour. Garnish, if desired. Serve with tortilla or pita chips. *Yield: 2 cups.*

Prep: 15 min., Chill: 1 hr.

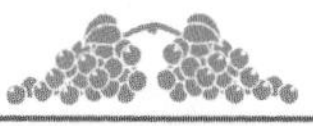

Recommended Wines

Beaujolais
Fumé Blanc

Caramelized Onion Tart

3 pounds large sweet onions, sliced
2 tablespoons olive oil
1 teaspoon salt
½ (17¼-ounce) package frozen puff pastry, thawed
½ cup shredded Parmesan cheese
Garnish: fresh rosemary sprigs

COOK onion in hot oil in a very large skillet or Dutch oven over low heat, stirring often, 30 to 35 minutes or until onion is caramel colored. Stir in salt, and set mixture aside.

UNFOLD pastry sheet; fit into a 9-inch square tart pan.

BAKE pastry at 400° for 15 to 20 minutes or until browned. Remove from oven. Press pastry with the back of a spoon to flatten. Top with caramelized onion; sprinkle with Parmesan cheese. Bake 5 more minutes. Garnish, if desired.

Yield: 6 servings.

Prep: 12 min., Cook: 35 min., Bake 25 min.

Recommended Wines

Merlot
Valpolicella

Pear, Jícama, and Snow Pea Salad

1 cup fresh snow pea pods
1 pear, peeled
1 small jícama, peeled
3/4 teaspoon lemon juice
1 (6-ounce) package baby spinach, sliced
1 (2-ounce) package sliced almonds, toasted
Vinaigrette (see opposite page)

COOK snow peas in boiling salted water to cover 30 seconds or until crisp-tender; drain. Plunge into ice water to stop the cooking process; drain.

CUT pea pods, pear, and jícama into thin strips; gently toss pear with lemon juice.

LAYER snow peas, pear, jícama, and spinach in a salad bowl; sprinkle with almonds. Serve with Vinaigrette. *Yield: 6 to 8 servings.*

Prep: 25 min., Cook: 30 sec.

Vinaigrette:

¼ cup balsamic vinegar
1 teaspoon Dijon mustard
1 garlic clove
1 teaspoon sugar
¼ teaspoon coarsely ground pepper
¾ cup olive oil
2 green onions, chopped
2 tablespoons fresh basil, chopped

PROCESS first 5 ingredients in a blender or food processor until smooth, stopping to scrape down sides. Gradually add olive oil in a slow, steady stream, and process mixture until well blended.

STIR in green onions and basil. Serve with salad.

Yield: ¾ cup.

Prep: 10 min.

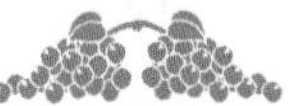

Recommended Wines

Pinot Grigio
Sauvignon Blanc

Wine has become a metaphor for the good life, a token of fellowship, an expression of romance.

GLORIA BLEY MILLER,
THE GIFT OF WINE

Veggie Sausage Pizzas

8 (1-inch-thick) French bread slices
1 sweet onion, sliced
1 medium-size green bell pepper, sliced
Vegetable cooking spray
1 cup tomato-and-basil pasta sauce
1 cup (4 ounces) shredded mozzarella cheese
1 (8-ounce) package meatless breakfast patties, thawed and crumbled
½ cup shredded Parmesan cheese

BAKE bread slices on a baking sheet at 425° for 5 minutes. Set aside.

SAUTÉ sliced onion and bell pepper in a large nonstick skillet coated with cooking spray over medium-high heat 5 minutes.

SPREAD pasta sauce evenly on 1 side of each bread slice. Top evenly with mozzarella cheese, onion mixture, crumbled patties, and Parmesan cheese.

BAKE at 425° for 10 minutes or until thoroughly heated. *Yield: 4 servings.*

Prep: 15 min., Bake: 15 min., Cook: 5 min.

RECOMMENDED WINE

Merlot

I know that wine is, above all else, a blessing, a gift of nature, a joy as pure and elemental as the soil and vines and sunshine from which it springs.

ROBERT MONDAVI,
HARVESTS OF JOY

Shellfish Crêpes in Wine-Cheese Sauce

½ cup butter or margarine, divided
2 cups chopped cooked shrimp (about 1 pound)
1 cup (8 ounces) fresh crabmeat
2 green onions, minced
¼ cup dry vermouth*
⅛ teaspoon salt
¼ teaspoon pepper
½ tablespoon butter or margarine, melted
Wine-Cheese Sauce (see page 50)
Crêpes (see page 51)
2 cups (8 ounces) shredded Swiss cheese
Garnish: sliced green onions

**Clam juice may be substituted for vermouth.*

MELT ¼ cup butter in a large skillet over medium-high heat. Add shrimp, crabmeat, and green onions, and sauté 1 minute. Stir in vermouth, salt, and pepper. Bring mixture to a boil, and cook 7 minutes or until most of liquid is absorbed. Remove mixture from heat, and set aside.

DRIZZLE ½ tablespoon melted butter into a 13- × 9-inch baking dish.

STIR 2 cups Wine-Cheese Sauce into shrimp mixture. Spoon about 3 tablespoons shrimp mixture down center of each Crêpe.

ROLL up, and place, seam side down, in prepared dish. Spoon remaining 2 cups Wine-Cheese Sauce over Crêpes. Sprinkle with Swiss cheese, and dot with remaining ¼ cup butter.

Cover and chill 3 hours. Let stand at room temperature 30 minutes.

BAKE at 450° for 20 minutes or until thoroughly heated. Garnish, if desired.

Yield: 12 servings.

Prep: 1 hr., Chill: 3 hrs., Stand: 30 min., Bake: 20 min.

Wine-Cheese Sauce:

- **¼ cup cornstarch**
- **¼ cup milk**
- **⅓ cup dry vermouth***
- **3 cups whipping cream**
- **¼ teaspoon salt**
- **¼ teaspoon pepper**
- **2 cups (8 ounces) shredded Swiss cheese**

**Clam juice may be substituted for vermouth.*

WHISK together cornstarch and milk in a small bowl.

BRING vermouth to a boil in a large skillet, and cook until vermouth is reduced to 1 tablespoon. Remove from heat, and whisk in cornstarch mixture. Add whipping cream, salt, and pepper; cook over medium-high heat, whisking constantly, 2 minutes or until mixture comes to a boil. Boil 1 minute or until mixture is thickened. Add Swiss cheese; reduce heat, and simmer, whisking constantly, 1 minute or until sauce is smooth. *Yield: 4 cups.*

Prep: 10 min., Cook: 10 min.

Wine is bottled poetry.

ROBERT LOUIS STEVENSON,
HARVESTS OF JOY

Crêpes:

- 4 large eggs
- 2 cups all-purpose flour
- ¼ cup butter or margarine, melted
- 1 cup cold water
- 1 cup cold milk
- ½ teaspoon salt

PROCESS all ingredients in a blender or food processor until smooth, stopping to scrape down sides. Cover and chill 1 hour.

PLACE a lightly greased 8-inch nonstick skillet over medium heat until skillet is hot.

POUR 3 tablespoons batter into skillet; quickly tilt in all directions so batter covers bottom of skillet.

COOK 1 minute or until Crêpe can be shaken loose from skillet. Turn Crêpe, and cook about 30 seconds. Repeat procedure with remaining batter. Stack Crêpes between sheets of wax paper. *Yield: 2 dozen.*

Prep: 8 min., Chill: 1 hr., Cook: 36 min.

Note: Assemble Shellfish Crêpes in Wine-Cheese Sauce a day ahead, if desired. Cover and chill. Let stand at room temperature 30 minutes before baking; proceed as directed.

RECOMMENDED WINE

Chardonnay

Lamb Chops With Mint Aïoli

6 garlic cloves, minced
2 teaspoons dried summer savory
1 teaspoon salt
1 teaspoon pepper
16 (2-inch-thick) lamb chops
1 tablespoon olive oil
Mint Aïoli (see opposite page)
Garnish: fresh mint sprigs

COMBINE first 4 ingredients, and rub evenly into both sides of lamb chops.

BROWN chops in hot oil in a large nonstick skillet over medium-high heat 2 to 3 minutes on each side. Arrange chops on a lightly greased rack in a broiler pan.

BAKE chops at 350° for 35 to 40 minutes or until a meat thermometer inserted into thickest portion registers 145° (medium rare). Serve lamb with Mint Aïoli. Garnish, if desired.

Yield: 6 to 8 servings.

Prep: 15 min., Bake: 40 min.

RECOMMENDED WINES

Merlot
Zinfandel

Mint Aïoli:

1 cup mayonnaise
¼ cup coarsely chopped fresh mint
4 garlic cloves, minced
1 teaspoon grated lemon rind
2 tablespoons fresh lemon juice
½ teaspoon salt
½ teaspoon pepper

PROCESS all ingredients in a blender or food processor until smooth, stopping to scrape down sides. *Yield: 1¼ cups.*

Prep: 5 min.

Glazed Salmon With Stir-Fried Vegetables

2 carrots
1 parsnip
1 small red bell pepper
8 green onions
4 (4-ounce) skinless salmon fillets
¼ teaspoon salt
Vegetable cooking spray
¼ cup apple jelly
3 tablespoons rice wine vinegar
2 tablespoons water
1 tablespoon soy sauce
1 teaspoon cornstarch
½ to 1 teaspoon chopped fresh dill (optional)
2 teaspoons vegetable oil
Garnish: fresh dill sprigs

CUT first 4 ingredients into thin strips, and set aside.

SPRINKLE salmon fillets evenly with salt. Place on a rack in a broiler pan coated with cooking spray.

BROIL 6 inches from heat 10 to 13 minutes or until fish flakes with a fork.

WHISK together jelly, next 4 ingredients, and, if desired, dill.

COOK carrot and parsnip in hot oil in a large skillet over medium-high heat, stirring often, 2 to 3 minutes. Add bell pepper and onions; cook 1 to 2 minutes or until crisp-tender. Remove vegetables from skillet, and keep warm.

ADD jelly mixture to skillet and cook, stirring constantly, 3 to 4 minutes or until thickened.

SPOON vegetables evenly onto serving plates. Drizzle with half of sauce. Top with salmon fillets, and drizzle with remaining sauce. Garnish, if desired. *Yield: 4 servings.*

Prep: 15 min., Cook: 22 min.

Recommended Wines

Pinot Noir
Rosé

Chicken-and-Sausage Jambalaya

1 (16-ounce) package Cajun-style smoked sausage, cut into ¼-inch slices
2 celery ribs, chopped
1 medium onion, chopped
1 medium-size green bell pepper, chopped
4 cups chopped cooked chicken*
1 (32-ounce) container chicken broth
1¼ cups uncooked long-grain rice
1 tablespoon Cajun seasoning
Garnish: chopped fresh parsley

**We used a deli chicken to make this entrée easier. Be sure to remove all skin and bones.*

COOK smoked sausage in a Dutch oven over medium heat, stirring constantly, 3 minutes or until browned. Add celery, onion, and bell pepper, and sauté 6 to 8 minutes or until vegetables are tender.

STIR in chicken and next 3 ingredients; bring to a boil. Cover, reduce heat, and simmer 45 minutes or until rice is done and liquid is absorbed. Remove from heat, and let stand 10 to 15 minutes before serving. Garnish, if desired.

Yield: 6 to 8 servings.

Prep: 20 min., Cook: 45 min., Stand: 15 min.

RECOMMENDED WINE

Zinfandel

In a disconnected world, wine connects. . . . It connects us to harvests long past, sunlight long faded, rain long soaked into the earth.

HEIDI YORKSHIRE, *SIMPLY WINE*

Smoked Pork Shoulder

1 (5- to 6-pound) pork shoulder or Boston butt pork roast
2 teaspoons salt
10 pounds hardwood charcoal, divided
Hickory wood chunks
Cider Vinegar Barbecue Sauce (see opposite page)

SPRINKLE pork with salt; cover and chill 30 minutes.

PREPARE charcoal fire with half of charcoal in grill; let burn 15 to 20 minutes or until covered with gray ash.

PUSH coals evenly into piles on both sides of grill. Carefully place 2 hickory chunks on top of each pile, and place food rack on grill.

PLACE pork, meaty side down, on rack directly in center of grill. Cover with lid, leaving ventilation holes completely open.

PREPARE an additional charcoal fire with 12 briquets in an auxiliary grill or fire bucket; let burn 30 minutes or until covered with gray ash. Carefully add 6 briquets to each pile in smoker; place 2 more hickory chunks on each pile. Repeat procedure every 30 minutes.

COOK, covered, 5 hours and 30 minutes or until meat thermometer inserted into thickest portion registers at least 165°, turning once the last 2 hours. (Cooking the pork to 165° makes the meat easier to remove from the bone.)

REMOVE pork; cool slightly. Chop and serve with Cider Vinegar Barbecue Sauce.

Yield: 6 servings.

Prep: 30 min., Chill: 30 min., Cook: 5½ hrs.

Cider Vinegar Barbecue Sauce:

1½ cups cider vinegar
⅓ cup firmly packed brown sugar
¼ cup ketchup
1 tablespoon hot sauce
1 teaspoon browning and seasoning sauce
½ teaspoon salt
½ teaspoon onion powder
½ teaspoon pepper
½ teaspoon Worcestershire sauce

STIR together all ingredients in a medium saucepan; cook over medium heat, stirring constantly, 7 minutes or until sugar dissolves. Cover and chill sauce until ready to serve. Serve with Smoked Pork Shoulder. *Yield: 2 cups.*

Prep: 10 min., Cook: 7 min.

RECOMMENDED WINES

Chianti
Zinfandel

Garlic-Rosemary Roasted Chicken With Potatoes

1 (5- to 6-pound) whole chicken
1 tablespoon chopped fresh rosemary
8 garlic cloves, crushed
2 tablespoons olive oil, divided
¼ teaspoon paprika
8 shallots or small onions
2 garlic bulbs
1½ pounds baking potatoes
3 tablespoons olive oil
¼ teaspoon salt
¼ teaspoon pepper
Garnish: fresh rosemary sprigs

LOOSEN skin from chicken breast and drumsticks by inserting fingers and gently pushing between the skin and meat. Place rosemary and crushed garlic beneath skin on breasts and drumsticks. Tie ends of legs together with string. Place chicken, breast side up, on a rack in a broiler pan. Brush chicken with 1 tablespoon olive oil, and sprinkle with paprika.

CUT a thin slice from each shallot. Remove skin, and cut off tops of garlic bulbs, leaving roots intact. Brush shallots and garlic with 1 tablespoon olive oil; arrange shallots and garlic around chicken. Bake, uncovered, at 450° for 30 minutes.

MEANWHILE, cut potatoes lengthwise into thin strips. Combine potato strips and next 3 ingredients in a large heavy-duty, zip-top plastic bag. Seal bag, and shake to coat. Remove potato strips from bag, and arrange in a single layer on a large baking sheet.

REDUCE temperature to 400°; add potatoes to lower oven rack. Bake chicken and potatoes at 400° for 35 minutes or until meat thermometer inserted in meaty part of thigh registers 180°, stirring potatoes after 15 minutes. Remove chicken from oven.

INCREASE oven temperature to broil. Broil potatoes 5½ inches from heat 12 to 15 minutes or until crisp and golden, stirring frequently. Place chicken on a serving platter and serve with roasted garlic, shallots, and potatoes. Garnish, if desired. *Yield: 6 to 8 servings.*

Prep: 22 min., Bake: 65 min., Broil: 15 min.

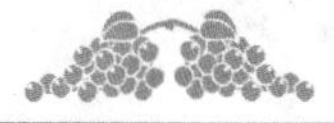

Recommended Wines

Chardonnay
Pinot Noir

Trout Amandine

2 tablespoons butter
⅓ cup sliced almonds
½ cup milk
1 egg yolk
½ teaspoon hot sauce
1 cup all-purpose flour
1 teaspoon salt
1 teaspoon pepper
6 (12-ounce) rainbow trout fillets
Vegetable oil
Lemon Cream Sauce (see opposite page)
Garnish: lemon wedges

MELT butter in a large heavy skillet over low heat; add almonds, and sauté until golden. Remove almonds from skillet; drain on paper towels. Wipe skillet clean.

WHISK together milk, egg yolk, and hot sauce in a shallow dish. Stir together flour, salt, and

pepper in a bowl. Dredge fillets in flour mixture; dip in egg mixture. Dredge fillets again in flour mixture, shaking to remove excess flour mixture.

POUR oil to a depth of ¼ inch into skillet; heat to 375°. Fry trout, in batches, 3 to 4 minutes on each side or until golden. Serve with Lemon Cream Sauce; sprinkle with almonds. Garnish, if desired. *Yield: 6 servings.*

Prep: 18 min., Cook: 8 min. (per batch)

Lemon Cream Sauce:

- **½ cup butter**
- **2 tablespoons all-purpose flour**
- **1 (14-ounce) can chicken broth**
- **2 garlic cloves, pressed**
- **1 tablespoon lemon juice**
- **⅓ cup whipping cream**
- **¼ cup white wine Worcestershire sauce**
- **¼ teaspoon salt**
- **½ teaspoon hot sauce**

MELT butter in a large skillet over medium heat; whisk in flour. Cook, whisking constantly, 1 minute. Whisk in broth, garlic, and lemon juice; bring to a boil, whisking constantly. Reduce heat, and simmer, whisking constantly, 5 minutes. Whisk in whipping cream and remaining ingredients, and cook, whisking constantly, 5 minutes or until thickened. *Yield: 1¼ cups.*

Prep: 3 min., Cook: 11 min.

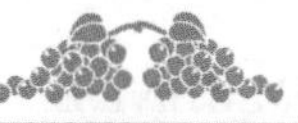

Recommended Wine

Chardonnay

Beef Fillets With Orange Cream

4 (6- to 8-ounce) beef tenderloin steaks
½ teaspoon cracked black pepper (optional)
1 cup whipping cream
2 tablespoons orange marmalade
1 to 2 tablespoons prepared horseradish
Garnish: orange rind curls

SPRINKLE steaks with cracked pepper, if desired.

GRILL steaks, covered with grill lid, over medium-hot coals (350° to 400°) 4 to 6 minutes on each side or to desired degree of doneness. Bring whipping cream, marmalade, and horseradish to a boil over medium-high heat, stirring constantly; reduce heat, and simmer 5 minutes or until thickened, stirring often. Serve immediately with steaks; garnish, if desired.

Yield: 4 servings.

Prep: 9 min., Grill: 12 min.

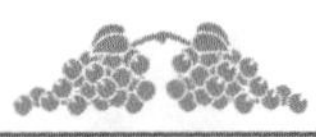

Recommended Wines

Chianti
Merlot

Strawberry-Almond Romanoff

1 quart fresh strawberries, halved
½ cup sugar
½ cup amaretto or other almond-flavored liqueur
1 cup whipping cream
2 tablespoons powdered sugar
1 teaspoon almond extract
Garnishes: toasted almond slices, fresh mint sprigs

STIR together first 3 ingredients. Cover and chill 3 hours.

BEAT whipping cream at medium speed with an electric mixer until foamy; gradually add powdered sugar and almond extract, beating until soft peaks form.

SPOON strawberry halves into stemmed glasses, and top with sweetened whipped cream. Garnish, if desired. *Yield: 4 servings.*

Prep: 25 min., Chill: 3 hrs.

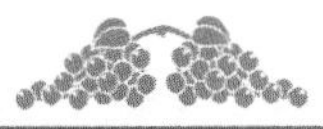

Recommended Wines

Italian sparkling wine
(try Asti, Prosecco, or Moscato d' Asti)

Blueberries and Cream Cheesecake

1½ cups graham cracker crumbs
1½ cups plus 2 tablespoons sugar, divided
⅓ cup butter or margarine, melted
3½ cups fresh blueberries, divided
3 tablespoons cornstarch, divided
3 (8-ounce) packages cream cheese, softened
4 large eggs
¼ teaspoon salt
2 (8-ounce) cartons sour cream
½ teaspoon vanilla extract
¼ cup water

STIR together graham cracker crumbs, ¼ cup sugar, and butter. Press mixture evenly in bottom and ½ inch up sides of a 9-inch springform pan. Bake at 325° for 9 minutes. Cool.

PROCESS 2½ cups blueberries and 1 tablespoon cornstarch in container of an electric blender until smooth, stopping once to scrape down sides. Pour into a saucepan. Cook over medium heat, stirring constantly, about 15 minutes or until slightly thickened. Set mixture aside to cool. Cover and chill ½ cup mixture for making glaze.

BEAT cream cheese at medium speed with an electric mixer until light and fluffy. Gradually add 1 cup sugar, mixing well. Add eggs, 1 at a time, beating after each addition. Stir in remaining 2 tablespoons cornstarch and salt. Pour batter into prepared pan. Pour blueberry mixture over batter; gently swirl with a knife. Bake at 325° for 45 minutes or until set. Remove from oven; cool on a wire rack 20 minutes.

STIR together sour cream, 2 tablespoons sugar, and vanilla; spread over cheesecake. Bake at 325° for 10 more minutes. Cool in pan on wire rack. Cover and chill 8 hours.

STIR together reserved ½ cup blueberry mixture, remaining ¼ cup sugar, and ¼ cup water in a small saucepan; cook over medium heat, stirring constantly, until thickened. Gently fold in remaining 1 cup blueberries; cool. Remove sides of springform pan. Spoon blueberry glaze over cheesecake. *Yield: 10 to 12 servings.*

Prep: 45 min., Bake: 64 min., Chill: 8 hrs.

Recommended Wines

Sherry
Sweet sparkling wine

Pear Dumplings

3 cups all-purpose flour
2 teaspoons baking powder
1 teaspoon salt
1 cup shortening
¾ cup milk
6 medium-size firm, ripe pears, such as Bosc or Bartlett
¼ cup firmly packed brown sugar
1 teaspoon ground cinnamon
½ cup chopped macadamia nuts
¼ cup cold butter or margarine, cut up
1½ cups sugar
1½ cups water
1 tablespoon butter or margarine
Rind of 1 medium-size orange, cut into strips
1 (3-inch) slice fresh ginger

COMBINE first 3 ingredients; cut in shortening with a pastry blender or two knives until mixture is crumbly. Gradually add milk, stirring to make a soft dough. Turn dough out onto a lightly floured surface, and roll into a 21- × 14-inch rectangle. Cut rectangle into 6 (7-inch) squares using a party wheel.

PEEL pears, reserving skin. Core each pear from bottom, leaving top 2 inches. Place each pear, bottom side down, on a pastry square.

STIR together brown sugar, cinnamon, and chopped nuts; spoon 2 teaspoonsful mixture into each pear core, pressing firmly. Dot tops of pears evenly with ¼ cup butter.

MOISTEN pastry edges with water. Bring corners to center, pinching edges to seal. Place

pear dumplings in a lightly greased 13- × 9-inch baking dish.

BAKE at 375° for 40 to 50 minutes, shielding with aluminum foil after 30 minutes to prevent excessive browning.

BRING reserved pear skin, 1½ cups sugar, and next 4 ingredients to a boil in a medium saucepan over medium-high heat. Reduce heat; simmer, stirring occasionally, 4 minutes or until butter melts and sugar dissolves. Remove from heat. Pour through a wire-mesh strainer into a bowl, discarding solids. Pour syrup over dumplings. Serve immediately. *Yield: 6 servings.*

Prep: 60 min., Bake: 50 min.

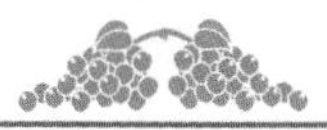

Recommended Wines

Muscat
Sweet sparkling wine

Coco Loco Custard

1½ cups sugar, divided
½ cup water
3 large eggs
2 egg yolks
2½ cups warm milk
½ cup sweetened flaked coconut, toasted
2 tablespoons dark rum
1 tablespoon vanilla extract
Garnish: toasted coconut

COMBINE 1 cup sugar and ½ cup water in a 9-inch cakepan; cook over low heat 10 minutes or until sugar caramelizes, tipping pan to cover bottom evenly.

WHISK together eggs, yolks, and remaining ½ cup sugar until blended. Gradually add milk, whisking constantly; stir in coconut, rum, and vanilla. Pour mixture into prepared pan. Cover with aluminum foil; place on a jellyroll pan. Add hot water to jellyroll pan to a depth of ¼ to ½ inch.

BAKE at 325° for 1 hour and 10 minutes or until a knife inserted in center comes out clean. Remove from water, and uncover; cool in cakepan on a wire rack. Cover and chill 3 hours.

RUN a knife around edge of custard to loosen; invert onto a serving plate. Garnish, if desired.

Yield: 8 servings.

Prep: 30 min., Bake: 1 hr., 10 min., Chill: 3 hrs.

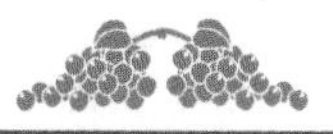

Recommended Wines

Madeira
Port

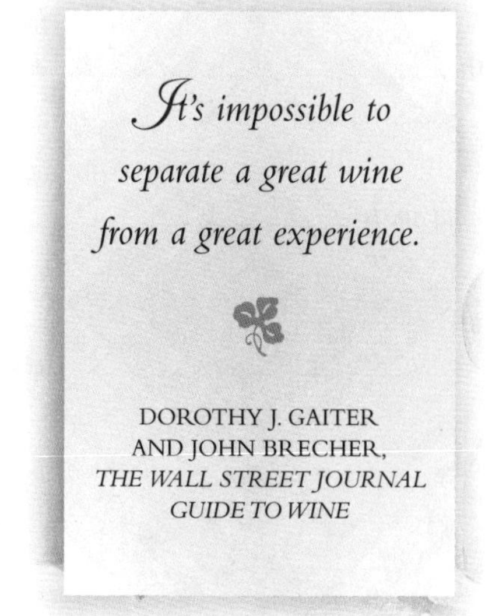

Wine ______________________

Purchased at ______________________

Price ____________ *Date* ____________

Producer ______________________

Vintage ______________________

Grape ______________________

Growing region ______________________

Vineyard ______________________

Impressions ______________________

____

____

Date opened ______________________

Served with ______________________

____

Guests shared with ______________________

____

Occasion ______________________

Wine ____________________

Purchased at ____________________

Price ____________ *Date* ____________

Producer ____________________

Vintage ____________________

Grape ____________________

Growing region ____________________

Vineyard ____________________

Impressions ____________________

____

____

Date opened ____________________

Served with ____________________

____

Guests shared with ____________________

____

Occasion ____________________

Always remember that today's unripe grape
will be tomorrow's prize.

MICHAEL LEE WEST, *CONSUMING PASSIONS*

Wine ________________________________

Purchased at ________________________________

Price ______________ *Date* ______________

Producer ________________________________

Vintage ________________________________

Grape ________________________________

Growing region ________________________________

Vineyard ________________________________

Impressions ________________________________

____

____

Date opened ________________________________

Served with ________________________________

____

Guests shared with ________________________________

____

Occasion ________________________________

The flavor of wine is like delicate poetry.

LOUIS PASTEUR

Wine ______________________

Purchased at ______________________

Price ____________ *Date* ____________

Producer ______________________

Vintage ______________________

Grape ______________________

Growing region ______________________

Vineyard ______________________

Impressions ______________________

____

____

Date opened ______________________

Served with ______________________

____

Guests shared with ______________________

____

Occasion ______________________

Wine ______

Purchased at ______

Price ______ *Date* ______

Producer ______

Vintage ______

Grape ______

Growing region ______

Vineyard ______

Impressions ______

______

______

Date opened ______

Served with ______

______

Guests shared with ______

______

Occasion ______

Wine ____________________

Purchased at ____________________

Price __________ *Date* __________

Producer ____________________

Vintage ____________________

Grape ____________________

Growing region ____________________

Vineyard ____________________

Impressions ____________________

____

____

Date opened ____________________

Served with ____________________

____

Guests shared with ____________________

____

Occasion ____________________

The discovery of wine is of greater moment
than the discovery of a constellation.
The universe is too full of stars.

ANTHELME BRILLAT-SAVARIN

Wine ____________________

Purchased at ____________________

Price ____________________ *Date* ____________________

Producer ____________________

Vintage ____________________

Grape ____________________

Growing region ____________________

Vineyard ____________________

Impressions ____________________

____

____

Date opened ____________________

Served with ____________________

____

Guests shared with ____________________

____

Occasion ____________________

A fine meal . . . is a delight in itself;
add a glass of wine—gleaming red or a translucent
greenish-gold—and delectation will be doubled.

ALEXIS LICHINE'S NEW ENCYCLOPEDIA
OF WINES AND SPIRITS

Wine ______________________

Purchased at ______________________

Price ____________ *Date* ____________

Producer ______________________

Vintage ______________________

Grape ______________________

Growing region ______________________

Vineyard ______________________

Impressions ______________________

____

____

Date opened ______________________

Served with ______________________

____

Guests shared with ______________________

____

Occasion ______________________

Wine ______________________

Purchased at ______________________

Price ____________ *Date* ____________

Producer ______________________

Vintage ______________________

Grape ______________________

Growing region ______________________

Vineyard ______________________

Impressions ______________________

____

____

Date opened ______________________

Served with ______________________

____

Guests shared with ______________________

____

Occasion ______________________

Wine ______________________

Purchased at ______________________

Price ____________ *Date* ____________

Producer ______________________

Vintage ______________________

Grape ______________________

Growing region ______________________

Vineyard ______________________

Impressions ______________________

____

____

Date opened ______________________

Served with ______________________

____

Guests shared with ______________________

____

Occasion ______________________

Wine gives great pleasure, and every pleasure is of itself a good.

SAMUEL JOHNSON

Wine ______________________

Purchased at ______________________

Price ____________ *Date* ____________

Producer ______________________

Vintage ______________________

Grape ______________________

Growing region ______________________

Vineyard ______________________

Impressions ______________________

____

____

Date opened ______________________

Served with ______________________

____

Guests shared with ______________________

____

Occasion ______________________

Wine is earth's answer to the sun.

MARGARET FULLER,
LETTERS FROM NEW-YORK, 2ND SERIES

Wine ____________________

Purchased at ____________________

Price __________ *Date* __________

Producer ____________________

Vintage ____________________

Grape ____________________

Growing region ____________________

Vineyard ____________________

Impressions ____________________

____

____

Date opened ____________________

Served with ____________________

____

Guests shared with ____________________

____

Occasion ____________________

Wine ______________________

Purchased at ______________________

Price ______________ *Date* ______________

Producer ______________________

Vintage ______________________

Grape ______________________

Growing region ______________________

Vineyard ______________________

Impressions ______________________

____

____

Date opened ______________________

Served with ______________________

____

Guests shared with ______________________

____

Occasion ______________________

From wine what sudden
friendship springs!

JOHN GAY, *FABLES*

Wine ______________________

Purchased at ______________________

Price ____________ *Date* ____________

Producer ______________________

Vintage ______________________

Grape ______________________

Growing region ______________________

Vineyard ______________________

Impressions ______________________

____

____

Date opened ______________________

Served with ______________________

____

Guests shared with ______________________

____

Occasion ______________________

Wine ______________________

Purchased at ______________________

Price ______________ *Date* ______________

Producer ______________________

Vintage ______________________

Grape ______________________

Growing region ______________________

Vineyard ______________________

Impressions ______________________

____

____

Date opened ______________________

Served with ______________________

____

Guests shared with ______________________

____

Occasion ______________________

Wine ________________________________

Purchased at ________________________________

Price ________________ *Date* ________________

Producer ________________________________

Vintage ________________________________

Grape ________________________________

Growing region ________________________________

Vineyard ________________________________

Impressions ________________________________

____

____

Date opened ________________________________

Served with ________________________________

____

Guests shared with ________________________________

____

Occasion ________________________________

A glorious wine, fragrant,
and full of gentle might;
a bottled-up happiness,
put by for use; a golden liquid,
worth more than liquid gold.

NATHANIEL HAWTHORNE,
THE HOUSE OF THE SEVEN GABLES

Wine ____________________

Purchased at ____________________

Price __________ *Date* __________

Producer ____________________

Vintage ____________________

Grape ____________________

Growing region ____________________

Vineyard ____________________

Impressions ____________________

____

____

Date opened ____________________

Served with ____________________

____

Guests shared with ____________________

____

Occasion ____________________

When it comes to eating
without my glass
of wine—I am nowhere.

JOSEPH CONRAD, *LORD JIM*

Wine ______________________

Purchased at ______________________

Price ____________ *Date* ____________

Producer ______________________

Vintage ______________________

Grape ______________________

Growing region ______________________

Vineyard ______________________

Impressions ______________________

____

____

Date opened ______________________

Served with ______________________

____

Guests shared with ______________________

____

Occasion ______________________

Wine ______________________

Purchased at ______________________

Price ____________ *Date* ____________

Producer ______________________

Vintage ______________________

Grape ______________________

Growing region ______________________

Vineyard ______________________

Impressions ______________________

____

____

Date opened ______________________

Served with ______________________

____

Guests shared with ______________________

____

Occasion ______________________

Wine ______________________

Purchased at ______________________

Price ______________ *Date* ______________

Producer ______________________

Vintage ______________________

Grape ______________________

Growing region ______________________

Vineyard ______________________

Impressions ______________________

____

____

Date opened ______________________

Served with ______________________

____

Guests shared with ______________________

____

Occasion ______________________

Joy is the best of wine.

GEORGE ELIOT, *SILAS MARNER*

Wine ______________________________

Purchased at ______________________________

Price ______________ *Date* ______________

Producer ______________________________

Vintage ______________________________

Grape ______________________________

Growing region ______________________________

Vineyard ______________________________

Impressions ______________________________

____

____

Date opened ______________________________

Served with ______________________________

____

Guests shared with ______________________________

____

Occasion ______________________________

Wine, one sip of this will bathe
the drooping spirits in delight beyond
the bliss of dreams. Be wise and taste.

JOHN MILTON